FROM ZERO TO TEN

The story of numbers

VIVIAN FRENCH
& ROSS COLLINS

CONTENTS

TWO – FOUR – SIX – EIGHT
What do we appreciate?

Numbers!!!!

Think about how often we use them.

"Help! I'm late!" "What's the time?"

"We won! Three-two! We won!"

"How much?"

"What year were you born?"

"Aren't we there yet?"

"How far is it?"

And all around us clocks are
ticking and computers are clicking...

What would shops, factories, hospitals, travellers, all of us, do without numbers?

So where did numbers come from?

HOW DID IT ALL BEGIN?

MAYBE PREHISTORIC men and women sitting in their caves boasted about how many animals they had killed, or told each other how many there were in an enemy attack...

"I caught so many fish, the river is empty!"
"Ugh! You caught fewer fish than I have noses!"
"The enemy came. They were like a swarm of bees!"
"Ugh! There were as many as the toes on my feet!"

But what if there had been 17 enemies on the mountain? Or 170? What if they had to hurry off to warn neighbouring families? How did people begin to count... and then remember how many they had counted?

The mammoths are coming!

How many?

I can't say.

How far away?

I can't say.

This isn't working...

7

HOW DO YOU COUNT WITHOUT NUMBERS?

THE EASIEST **COUNTING MACHINE** to use is your hand – the very first calculator! With two hands you have eight fingers and two thumbs: ten! And you can count your toes as well... twenty!

So, people began to count on their fingers. Very useful – but what about sending messages? You can't send your fingers...

Suppose you sent your little brother to buy four pigs. You could show him four on his fingers, or you could say "as many as the legs on a pig". But he might forget!

One pebble stands for one pig!

You could give him four pebbles, then he could check – one pebble for each pig. He could even leave the four pebbles with the pigs' owner. Then the owner would have a receipt or a record of how many pigs had gone – one pebble for each pig!

P.S. And don't think the sophisticated mathematicians of today have left pebbles behind. The word 'calculate' comes straight from the Latin word calculus... Which means what? Yes – pebble!

On second thoughts... forget the receipt.

One mark stands for one dead pig!

Another way of recording numbers is to make marks. There are still marks on cave walls showing how many animals the cave people killed... At least, that's what we think the marks mean. They *might* show how many hot dinners people had eaten, or how many times their mum nagged them to clear up the bones. Some people made marks on sticks. These are called tally sticks.

In Czechoslovakia, a wolf bone was found with 55 notches. An even older stick was found in the Lebembo Mountains in Africa. It is more than 37,000 years old! Who was its owner and what was she counting?

Tally sticks may seem old fashioned, but they were still being used up to recently. You see, you can't cheat with a tally stick: a shopkeeper can take two sticks, and mark both each time he sells something. He keeps one tally stick, and the customer keeps the other – like a receipt!

And one knot stands for one sweet

The **INCAS** of South America counted by tying knots in a piece of string. How many sweets do you eat in a week? Try keeping count – pebbles, notches on a stick, knots on a string... Can you think of any other ways?

So why don't we still count like this, or with pebbles? Think about larger numbers. How many sweets do you eat in a year? Could you carry that many pebbles? And if you used string, maybe you'd run out of string... or tie yourself up. There has to be a simpler way of dealing with large numbers.

He said I could get an exchange if I kept the receipt!

I'm totally squashed!

No more cakes!

HOW DO YOU COUNT BIG NUMBERS?

IMAGINE ANOTHER BOY going to market. He's carrying six pebbles to remind him to buy six apples. Simple!

Then out pops Grandma, "If you're going to market, dearie, you can fetch me some apples. I'd like this many." And she hands him lots of pebbles. He can't carry them all! Something has to be done.

22 pebbles stand for 22 eggs

Look at the boy below and guess how many pebbles he has. Now count them – how did you do?

Look at the rest of the picture: glance at the trees then cover them with your hand – guess how many apples, then how many rabbits, how many clouds... Why is it so difficult?

It's because our brains get muddled if we see more than four things at once... if there's more than four we have to count.

Putting things in heaps helps

The little girl is clever. She's put her pebbles in little heaps of five. Now guess how many she's got? This time it's easier: because you know each heap has five pebbles, you can quickly work out that four groups of five make twenty, plus two left over makes twenty-two.

But how would this help the boy? Well, say he also put his pebbles in heaps of five, then used something to stand for each heap – maybe he used a shell...

One shell stands for five pebbles

So, one shell stands for five pebbles; five shells and two pebbles stand for twenty-two. Now, when the boy reaches the market he'll be able to remember how many apples he needs. And he doesn't have to carry twenty-two pebbles all the way! Hurrah!

He's made a huge mathematical leap... he's using something we call base.

Did you bring the shopping list?

?

I thought you had it!

Using 'base'

The number of pebbles you have in each heap is your base number. If, like the girl, you have 5, then you are using base 5.

The Ancient Egyptians used a base 10 counting system nearly 5,000 years ago. Most peoples have chosen 10 as their base number. Why?

Well, isn't it obvious? We've got a ready-made counting aid on the end of each arm. And 5 + 5 = 10.

But, some people, like the **MAYANS,** chose 20 – fingers and toes – while others have used small numbers like 4, or 2, or larger numbers like 12.

The Sumerians invented and counted in base 60. The Babylonians did too.

No one is quite certain why they chose 60 – but we do know that they were really *brilliant* at maths... they had to be!

Pause for very difficult question now: we still use base 60 every day – can you guess when? (Clue, you have one minute and two seconds to answer this question!)

EVERYTHING IN THE RIGHT PLACE!

THE NEXT STAGE came when people wanted to use even larger numbers.

Have a look at this Indian girl. She's using base 10 – so she works in heaps of tens: one shell stands for 10 pebbles. (History doesn't tell us what happened when an Indian trader using base 10 met a Babylonian shopkeeper using base 60. How did they work out the change?)

This girl has two grandmothers... and an aunt... and a next-door neighbour... And they all want apples! What is she going to do?

Ones on the right, tens on the left

Instead of just putting everything in heaps, she arranges the pebbles and shells very carefully – she puts shells on the left and pebbles on the right.

Each time the pebbles come to 10, she swaps them for a shell (one shell stands for 10 pebbles). Then she puts the shell on the left – this is the proper place for shells!

Wow!! She's discovered something really exciting – what you use doesn't matter at all. It's putting things in the right place that's really important! Yippeee!! She's discovered place value.

There's a place for hundreds too

Of course you can use more than two places. If there are too many aunts, the girl may end up with more than 99 pebbles. Then she can make a third place for hundreds!

Stop playing and get our apples!

But I've just invented place value...

12

Look at the birds. Toucan is collecting apples. Every time he has 10 he takes them in a basket to Chicken who's making apple pies.

10 apples in one pie

Chicken puts 10 apples in each pie... and Penguin eats 10 pies at a time... so, one fat Penguin = 10 pies... or 100 apples! HURRAH!!

Can you work out how many apples there are altogether?

The answer is in the glossary.

Place value is very important

Think about it. What's the difference between 12 and 21? If you put the 1 or the 2 the other way around, you get a totally different number.

Look at 3 and 42 and then 516. How do we know how much these numbers stand for? By looking at the place the numbers are in!

13

NOTHING MATTERS NOW!

ONCE PEOPLE HAD discovered base and place value, mathematics was well on its way. So, what else was needed?

NOTHING. What????

Exactly that. Nothing. You see, it's all very well having 1,2,3,4,5,6,7,8 and 9 – you can write forty-three: 43, or thirty-two: 32.

But what if you had three hundred and four – 3 in the place for hundreds, nothing in the place for tens and 4 in the place for ones (3 4) but someone might think it was only thirty-four!

Using something to mean nothing

What could be done? No one had the answer – even the very mathematical Babylonians seem to have just left spaces where there are no numbers.

Maybe at first, **INDIAN MATHEMATICIANS** left spaces like the Babylonians, but (perhaps because they kept getting their sums wrong) then they began to use a sign.

In the beginning the sign for nothing may have been a dot. A poet at the end of the 6th century described stars as "zero dots, scattered in the sky..." The dot gradually turned into a circle, which was easier to see. The word zero comes from the Sanskrit word 'shûnya' which means nothing.

In fact, zero wasn't a regular part of the counting system of any culture until about **5 CE**. The earliest date when we have definite records of it comes from an Indian manuscript called **LOKAVIBHAGA** from 458 CE.

What zero?

Zero, how beautiful!

You can't do this with a two!

By 8 CE the Arabs had borrowed the Indians' zero, and from Arabia it went to Europe...

But the Europeans didn't use it properly until 12 CE and it caused a great deal of confusion. No one quite knew what it was. How could it be a number? Surely if it was nothing, then it didn't mean anything!

In the end **LEONARDO OF PISA,** an Italian monk, made it clear in a mathematical text book written in 1202. He said that zero was a 'place holder', a sign to separate figures.

So – what difference does zero make? It completes the system of symbols – 123456789 – to give us 10.

Get the van, boys, we're taking this baby to Europe!

It's like nothing I've ever seen!

Think about 1 and 10...
Because the 0 pushes the 1 into the left-hand place (the place for tens) we're back with place value...

That little magic 0 means that 100, 1,000 and even 10,000 can be written and understood.

Nothing can be very important!

ARABIC NUMBERS

WE KNOW THE WORDS ten and twenty so well that we don't even think about them – but in the beginning there were no words for any numbers. Instead of 'one', a word like 'sun' or 'nose' might be used (you only ever see one sun; noses usually come one at a time!) For 'two' you could use 'wings' or 'ears'. Try inventing your own counting words up to ten.

Nowadays, we have special 'number words' which we keep for numbers: one, two, three... What is very interesting is how our words for the first few numbers are so similar in so many languages.

Take three. In English, French, Italian, Irish, German, Polish, Spanish and Lithuanian the number is three, trois, tre, trí, drei, trzy, tres, and trys.

Zero to ten from India

These number words are alike because they all developed from a very old language, Sanskrit, from Northern India. In Sanskrit, the word for three is 'tri'! And guess what – the numbers themselves come from India too.

Indian mathematicians began using nine **DIGITS** and zero long long before anyone else. One very learned astrologer-mathematician called **BRAHMAGUPTA** (628 CE) described it all in a book – this is the earliest written evidence of the digits.

From India to Arabia

Then in 776 CE a number of Indian scholars travelled to the Arabian court of the caliph al-Mansur. The **ARAB MATHEMATICIANS** there were very impressed with the Indian system and a little later, an Arab scholar called al-Khuwarizmi wrote about it in a book called *The Book of Addition and Subtraction by Indian Methods*.

This is the first known Arabic book showing Indian numbers and place value in detail. (This is why we say our numbers are *Arabic* even though they originally came from India!)

When the Arabic scholars began to use the Indian numbers, they adapted them to the way they liked to write. However, even though Arabic writing goes from left to right, they kept the Indian way of writing numbers from right to left – remember, ones on the right, tens on the left...

From Arabia to Europe – almost...

Al-Khuwarizmi's book was translated into Latin by **GERALDUS CREMONENSIS,** and this should have led to the new system being used in Europe, but the Europeans still did not want to use it.

Around 972 CE, another scholar, the French mathematician **GERBERT OF AURILLAC,** tried again to introduce the Indian numbers into Europe. But, even though he was made Pope Sylvester II in 999 CE, the Europeans remained suspicious of the foreign system.

The Europeans were still using Greek letters and the old Roman numerals (which look like tally-stick marks). But these were difficult to use and they made doing maths ever so complicated – people had to go to counting specialists to help them to work out even very simple addition. The Indian system was much easier –

you didn't need to use an abacus or anything else. You could just work with the numbers themselves. Even so, it was not until the end of the 14th century that merchants in England and Northern Europe finally used it.

All over the world!!

Now, however, everyone knows that this system of counting has been the most successful intellectual innovation ever made on our planet. It has spread and been adopted almost universally, far more extensively even than the letters of the alphabet which we now use. It is the nearest thing we have to a universal language!

17

HOW MUCH?

ONCE PEOPLE had learnt what numbers were, and how to make them work, they got to the fun bit. (Truly!) They could learn to *use* numbers. (And that *doesn't* just mean maths.)

There are so many different things we do every day that involve numbers, but we take it for granted and don't always notice just how clever we are!

Look at a handful of coins. You can probably add up how much they come to quite quickly – but would a friendly Martian be able to if she didn't know how they worked? She might think the lightest coins were worth the least, and the heaviest coins the most.

Or she might look at the marks on the coins: 1, 10, 50 – (AHA!! base and place value important here!) and maybe work out that 10 of this sort of coin = 5 of those sort of coins... But she still wouldn't know if the coins will buy her a helicopter or a peanut.

Shopping by swapping

In the beginning there were no coins or bank notes. Trade was done through swapping or bartering. "I'll swap 3 rabbits for your sheep." "What????? For my beautiful Fluffy? I want at least 100 rabbits!"

But supposing the owner of the rabbits didn't want a sheep at all? What if he wanted corn? Fluffy's owner would have to find someone to swap corn for Fluffy, then swap the corn for the rabbits!!! He could spend days or weeks looking for the right swap...

One token stands for one frog

As trading became more complicated, people began to use tokens instead. This was important – it meant that corn, or sheep, or pigs could be given a fixed value, or a 'market price'.

If Fluffy's owner knew that Fluffy was worth 24 tokens and the owner of the rabbit knew each rabbit was worth 6 tokens, they could work out how many rabbits to exchange for Fluffy. (Can you work it out?)

Native Americans like the Iroquois used strings of shells called 'wampum' as tokens. Cloth, pots, jewels, and animal teeth, horns and skins also became basic units for trade.

I've got hutches.

Don't you have anything else?

Are you sure these things are all wampum?

But what is it worth?

By the seventh century CE, Greece and China were making coins to use as tokens. The Chinese coins were made from iron and were very heavy. At first the metal coins were worth the weight of the metal – so a big gold coin was worth more than a little gold coin! But gradually, coins began to stand for a fixed amount.

We know a 20p coin is worth more than a 10p coin, even though it's smaller!

But there are always problems. Things don't stay the same value for ever. Think about Fluffy.

When there are not many sheep, Fluffy is worth a lot, but if there are hundreds of sheep, Fluffy won't be worth very much at all. BAAAAAA!!!! This is called depreciation.

It can work the other way too. Imagine you bought Fluffy for one gold coin when there were *lots* of sheep.

Don't sell him yet. Wait until sheep are very rare – Then sell him. WOW!! Five gold coins!

Metal money wasn't always very easy to handle. Iron coins were so heavy that shoppers began to leave them with the shopkeepers and use the paper receipts instead. Guess what? Paper money had been invented!!! When it first appeared the Chinese called paper money 'flying money' because of its tendency to blow away!

Now, we use something else as well as paper money and coins – plastic! The first **CREDIT CARD** was the Diners Card in 1950.

I might not have any change.

Sorry mate!

We buy and sell old sheep

I'll take it!

19

USING OUR BODIES TO MEASURE

SUPPOSE YOU WANT A PEN for Fluffy to live in? You'd need to find out how long Fluffy is – one sheep long?

Or as long as your outstretched arms... AHA! We've begun to measure.

When measuring began, the body was the obvious place to start.

The Egyptians used the cubit (the distance from the elbow to the tip of the middle finger) or span (from the top of your thumb to the tip of your little finger). This should be half a cubit – measure yourself and see!

In 1492, Leonardo da Vinci discovered that twice the measure of a man's wrist equals his neck; twice his neck equals his waist and, most curious of all, his two outstretched arms equal his height! Or...

2 wrists = 1 neck, 2 necks = 1 waist

2 arms = 1 man's height

So the ratio of the parts of the body is 2 to 1 (check out your body ratios). But does this actually help when it comes to measuring things? NO... Fluffy's pen may need to be twice as long as you are tall, but we need to know how long that is!

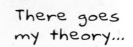

There goes my theory...

Words for collections of things

But it wasn't only distances that needed measuring. As trade increased, traders needed to know what to ask for. You can't count rice – one grain, two grains... fifteen thousand and seven grains... So, maybe they could ask for a bowl of rice: a measurement of *quantity*.

Once again, words related to the body were used: like pinches and handfuls, fists, bunches, armfuls and heaps. Or the words referred to the container – bags and sacks or gallons and buckets.

Wines and spirits were measured in hogsheads, pipes, butts, firkins and puncheons.

Some measures were very interesting: a fother was as much hay as one horse could pull in a cart.
Can you think of any new words for measuring things?

Special words for special jobs

Many trades developed their own system of measuring: paper came in sheets, quires and reams... (two reams made a bundle) and came in different sizes: Emperor, Antiquarian, Double Elephant, Atlas, Colombier, Imperial.

(This makes the modern A3 and A4 sound very dull – wouldn't you rather draw on an Elephant?)

Fishermen had all sorts of brilliant words for different quantities of fish: for example, 600 herrings = a mease, but 615 = a maze!

Here's a maths problem from a 1900 school book: If A bought a wash of oysters and sold them to B at so much per strike, what would be the price of a prickle of whelks?

Confusing? Yes, and hard to remember! What we need is a fixed measure or standard.

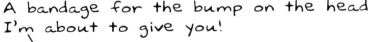

A spuckle of milk,
A work of winkles,
A flump of sausages,
An ouch of safety pins,
A jumple of wumples,
A foodle of snoodles,
Have I forgotten anything?

A bandage for the bump on the head
I'm about to give you!

STANDARDISATION

BUT, SINCE OUR BODIES are such different shapes and sizes, they make unreliable tools for measuring. People began to look for other things which were more likely to always be the same size or standard.

In China, a standard measure for rice was set in 221 BCE. The bowl used to measure grain had to be of a certain weight – and also make a particular ringing tone when struck!

Inches and pints

The British Imperial system of measurement was based on that used by European traders in the Middle Ages: inches, pounds and pints. These measures were set by the **MAGNA CARTA** in 1215 CE. But the system was not very easy to use since it had different units for length, weight, volume...

Elsewhere, people were developing other systems – Argentina, Mexico, and Turkey were among many countries that developed a system using base 10 long before it became a standard international measure.

12 inches = 1 foot
3 feet = 1 yard
1760 yards = 1 mile
16 ounces = 1 pound
14 pounds = 1 stone
160 stone = 1 ton
4 gills = 1 pint
2 pints = 1 quart
4 quarts = 1 gallon

Still using European hat sizes I see.

What's so heavy over there?

No thanks, we'll stick with base ten.

clear as mud!

Metres and litres

In 1799, France adopted the metric system. It was neat, rational, and *much* easier to use. Why? It's based on – yes, you guessed it – base 10!!!!!!

For measuring length:
10 millimetres = 1 centimetre
100 centimetres = 1 metre
1,000 metres = 1 kilometre

Or if you're measuring liquids:
1,000 millilitres = 1 litre
Or weights: milligrams, grams and kilograms!

The metric system was so neat that lots of other countries began to use it – or bits of it. BUT... you guessed it, not everyone did!

2 equals 4 equals 35????

Have you noticed that trainers often have lots of different sizes inside? This is because the UK, US and Europe still use different systems: so a UK 2 is a USA 4 and a European 35!!

And if you want a track suit, it's even worse – we're back with the body again! Most labels give ages (though some do have inches and centimetres as well). Do the makers really believe that all 9 year olds are the same size... in all countries... all over the world??

But at least when you finally find a pair of trainers and a track suit that fit perfectly and you race out onto the track, the 100 metres is the same the world over – even if you do have to use base 60 to figure out how fast you've run it!!

It's just me and my writing paper...

Dear Dad,
I'm in another book now

You'll grow into them...

Bong!

23

NUMBERS TO PLAY WITH

QUESTION: If you were running the 100 metres in Siberia in 1896, how far would you run? Answer: 100 metres. Unless you were a Martian! The metric system has been used for track events all over the world ever since the first modern Olympics. When was that? Yes! 1896. The Siberians might have been confused by the marathon though. That was 26 miles...

Over the years, the Olympic Committee has adopted the metric system for all events. This means that they can compare athletes' performances all over the world and from one year to another.

Since then, athletes and spectators alike have been as interested in breaking records as they have in winning races. And of course, as timing equipment has got more sophisticated (one hundredth of a second can now be measured accurately) every little improvement can be celebrated.

Fastest time wins!

Running races depend on measuring the speed at which the distance is run (the 100m record is under 10 seconds – that's 10 metres per second – while the 1,500 metres record is over 3 minutes or 8 metres per second).

Longest distance wins!

In field events like long and high jump, the height or length is important, not the speed. For the long jump, it's the longest of three jumps, for the high jump, it's not just the height but the person who gets the highest jump first time.

Highest SCORE wins!

Of course distance and speed are not the only things we measure in sport – most team games are based on scoring points. In soccer or basketball, when a player gets the ball into the goal or the basket, the team scores. And the team with the highest score wins.

24

Overs, tries, touchdowns, aces, conversions, runs, sets and birdies!

With games like rugby or American football, there are points for getting goals but also for other things like carrying the ball over the goal line.

And what about tennis? The points go 15, 30, 40 and then you win – but when the score is 40 all, it's *deuce*. Why? Because either player must now get *two* points in a row to win.

To win at cricket your team has to be the one with the most 'runs'. One team's bowler throws the ball. The batsman from the other team hits it, then runs from one fixed point to another before a 'fielder' from the bowler's team throws the ball back.

Complicated? Yes – and it gets worse. If you hit the ball hard enough you can score six runs and don't have to do any running at all... PHEW!!! Anyone for tennis?

Points for difficult moves

In some sports, the player gets points for performing feats which have different levels of technical difficulty. In diving, gymnastics and ice skating for example, points are awarded for the difficulty of the dive or jump and also for presentation – you don't have to just perform the jump, you have to look good as well!!

Lucky breaks

Of course not all games are about running and jumping – we use numbers to work out scores and points in all sorts of games. Most board games like chess or draughts involve travelling along squares on a board and getting points (or losing or gaining pieces) by making particular moves.

Some board games use dice. This means that as well as having the skill, the player needs to be lucky to win.

Anyone for snookis?

My skating may stink but look at this smile!

Home
395
Visitors
-2

25

LUCKY NUMBERS

THINK OF A NUMBER... do you have a lucky number? When fifty people were asked what their lucky number was, more than a third said seven!!!!

As well as standing for quantities, numbers have had other meanings for thousands of years. Think about three, and "third time lucky?" – but what about 13? No one has 13 as their lucky number; it is thought of as unlucky, and not just in the Christian tradition (Judas was the thirteenth disciple, and he betrayed Jesus). In Turkey it is thought terrible luck to mention 13; in Paris you would have to look very hard indeed to find a house numbered 13.

2,500 years ago, the Greek philosopher Pythagoras declared that there were good and bad numbers. For example, he thought 1 (unity) was a good number; but 2 (division) was bad.

Auspicious days!

Some people don't give fixed meanings to numbers – numbers are lucky or unlucky for you at different times. People who believe in astrology say that everything depends on the the day you were born and they often ask astrologers to help them decide when is a lucky day to do important things like move house or get married – or even to decide on who to marry!

Maybe you feel your lucky number is the date of your birthday and you notice that important things happen or that lots of famous people also have that birthday – or is it that you notice because it's yours?

Magic numbers!

Numbers have always been associated with magic – try this trick...
Write a number 6 on a piece of card, then put it in an envelope and seal it. Give your envelope to a friend. Then ask your friend to think of a number; tell them to double it; add 20; subtract 8; divide by 2, then subtract the number they thought of first... now open the envelope!

Palindromes (numbers that are the same backwards and forwards) are quite magical. Take the time at twenty one minutes past twelve (12:21) or the 10th of February 2001 (10/02/2001). Imagine if you were born on a palindromic date and your name was Anna or Bob!

Most magical of all were the twins who were born in Berlin – one just before midnight on the 31st December 1999, one born in the morning of 1st January 2000 – twins with birthdays in two different millennia!

IT'S COUNTDOWN TIME!

PERHAPS THE MOST important thing numbers are used for is to measure time. Trying to understand time may be what made our ancestors begin to use numbers in the first place.

You could start with a day: but should you measure from sunrise to sunrise, from sunset to sunset, from noon to noon, or from midnight to midnight?

Using the moon's cycle

If you measured from midnight to midnight and you watched the moon closely, you would notice that it had a regular 29-and-a-half-day cycle (the **LUNAR CYCLE**) – perfect for measuring long amounts of time, months even!

For nomadic peoples, the moon's cycle was perfect for measuring time. However, for people whose lives depended on raising crops (and predicting the seasons) the moon's cycles were not so useful. You couldn't tell when it was time to sow your seeds using moon time.

Using the sun's cycle

Almost 6,000 years ago, the Egyptians living along the river Nile found that the floods had a cycle, but one that was caused by the sun, not the moon.

Egyptian astronomers began to use the sun's cycle (the solar cycle). They worked out that it was 365 and a quarter days, and they solved the problem of the extra bit by inserting an extra day every four years – a leap year!

It's time we were leaving!

Gotta go before the flood!

It's a LEAP YEAR!

Blast off is at zero hundred hours!

28

If you know that the solar year is 365 and one quarter days, you don't have to be brilliant at sums to work out that 12 lunar months of 29 or 30 days only add up to 354, NOT 365. So, how can you make a sensible calendar?

The Julian Calendar

In 46 BCE **JULIUS CAESAR** borrowed the Egyptian's calendar to reform the Roman lunar one. He used the leap year idea, and added two extra months so the old Roman Lunar calendar could catch up with the new one – this year became known as the Year of Confusion (but at least he got the month of July called after him!).

To be *totally* accurate, the solar year is actually 365 days, 5 hours, 48 minutes and 46 seconds! One leap year every four years is too often – it puts in 11 minutes and 14 seconds too many. This doesn't sound much, but it adds up to one whole day every 128 years. It didn't bother Caesar, but after a thousand years, the months were out of line with the seasons again.

The Gregorian Calendar – ours!

In the 1570s **POPE GREGORY XIII** set up a commission to investigate and it was agreed that having a leap year only in three of every four century years ending in 00 would fix it.

This calendar is used widely around the world today. Some countries just use the Gregorian calendar for work and government: India adopted it in 1957 but kept the Hindu calendar for religious festivals. China adopted the Gregorian calendar in 1912 but continues to celebrate Chinese New Year in February (by Gregorian time).

Time to party!

January 1st, 2000, was a very special New Year and most people celebrated the new millennium. Or maybe it was just a good excuse for a party!!!

If you had a festival what would you celebrate? Maybe the world should all celebrate al-Khuwarizmi's birthday since he gave us our numbers... What about a party in 2345 CE? See you there!

29

GLOSSARY

ARAB MATHEMATICIANS

The 800 years from the 7th to the 15th century were a golden age of Muslim science and art. Inspired by their holy book, the *Qu'ran*, Arab scholars aspired to record every piece of knowledge gained by humankind and to advance it further. They set up libraries and research institutes, translating from Syrian, Persian, Chinese, Greek, Indian and other languages. Their most famous mathematician was al-Khuwarizmi. At the House of Wisdom in Baghdad (a centre of scientific research set up by the caliph al-Mumun) he worked on the books brought to the court by earlier Indian scholars and wrote his own books.

BCE

This stands for 'Before the Common Era'. Until recently, the term BC (Before Christ) was used, but since not everyone is a Christian we now use BCE instead – though the era still starts with the year 0, the year Christ is thought to have been born (see also CE).

BRAHMAGUPTA

This was an Indian mathematician of the 6th century who used the place value system and the nine numerals. He described how to do sums much as you learn to do them today and his books were used by the Arabs to develop mathematics even further.

CE

This stands for 'Common Era'. Until recently the term AD (*Anno Domini* which means 'the year of our Lord' in Latin) was used. However, not everyone in the world is Christian, so now the International Dating System uses CE instead (see also BCE).

COUNTING MACHINES

The first counting machine was the human body, especially the fingers. People have also knotted string, marked notches on tally sticks and so on. All over the world people have used different kinds of abacus (on the front of this book, the penguin is holding a Chinese one). You put stones or shells of different values on different sticks or in different compartments in order to do sums. An abacus is actually a calculator (the word just means counting machine) though nowadays we usually use the word to describe an electronic, hand-held counting machine.

CREDIT CARDS

These are cards issued by banks and shops which allow you to spend money and pay later. Usually you get a monthly bill, but often you only have to pay off a small amount of what you owe to be able to continue using your card.

DIGITS

A digit is any one of the ten numerals we use from 0 to 9. The word comes from the Latin word for 'finger'.

GERALDUS CREMONENSIS

He translated al-Khuwarizmi's books into Latin, introducing the Indian place value system and numerals to Europe.

GERBERT OF AURILLAC

When he lived in Spain, this French monk met many Arab mathematicians and brought back their ideas. Even with the importance he gained from being Pope, he still wasn't able to convince other Europeans to accept the Arabic system of numbers. Also, he didn't bring back the idea of zero, even though the Arabs had already learned it from the Indians.

INCAS

These native South American people are famous for their 'quipus' – a counting system using knots in pieces of string. Though they did not have a written language, they used quipus to set up a system of taxation and government which was very complex and efficient.

INDIAN MATHEMATICIANS

Mathematics, and all kinds of learning, flourished in the reign of the Gupta Dynasty whose empire stretched along the river Ganges from 240 to about 535 CE. At this time, Sanskrit, the ancient language of India, was developing and many important texts were written. They show that for Indian scholars numbers played an important religious and spiritual role. They had to find a way